Your Complete Guide To Make Money Online

Learn internet marketing strategies for 2015

Robert B. Newhall

Table of Contents

SECTION 1: HOW TO GENERATE INCOME OVER INTERNET

Chapter 1: Different Ways To Make Money Online

The internet has become quite a powerful tool that has been used to a large extent by organizations and business entities to pursue their profit ventures. Every individual wants to make an extra penny now and then. Thanks to the internet, this has stopped being a dream and is now the reality.

Using the internet as a money making platform has ceased to be a reserve of big companies. Individuals have now come up with several ways in which they can use the "free" platform to make money. Just consider the amount of time you spend every day on the internet surfing through social media websites and all other sorts of web pages.

Well, you can make better use of that time and earn some cash while enjoying browsing the internet. Unlike being employed, the internet allows you to determine the amount of money you can make in a day or even in an hour. I bet you already have a laptop or a tablet and a way of accessing the internet. What could you possibly be missing?

So you just haven't figured out the ways in which you can make money online, no problem. This article is tailored to provide you with an array of ways you can utilize the internet profitably. Here are a few easy ways that you just have to try.

1. Paid Writing

You will be shocked to discover just how much your writing skills can earn you over the internet. There are a large number of individuals out there who seek quality content on their web pages. As such, platforms have come up that allow you to provide relevant content to those individuals for a price.

The demand for quality articles, blog posts, academic scripts, and essays has been on the rise. This is probably due to the extensive research being conducted in various disciplines worldwide. Paid writing can earn you about $20 to $30 an hour.

Some individuals have greatly benefited from online writing and have been able to support themselves and their families. As if the earnings are not enough of an enticement, these online writing accounts are very easy to open and are basically free.

2. Selling Your Products

You don't have to be a multi-million dollar company in order to sell products online. This is a common fallacy that has misled a good number of individuals to limiting themselves to local markets. The internet is filled with hundreds of thousands of online shoppers looking for pretty much anything.

If you are selling electronics, beauty products, scrap, used cars, art, pets or clothes you will find that the internet is quite the ideal place to sell your products. Some online platforms will even allow you to put up your products for free.

With the internet, you can be guaranteed of improved profit margins due to the increased sales. You will also benefit greatly from expanding your brand visibility which will subsequently lead to newer markets for your products.

3. Create Your Own Website

This is probably one of the most profitable ways of utilizing the internet. Try to think of the number of times you have visited a certain web page only to be ushered by a number of ads. This might have annoyed you, but think of it from a money making perspective.

The ads generate a lot of money for the website owner. With the evolution of pay-per-view and pay-per-click, the Internet has become a goldmine for website owners. You need to design your website or have an expert do it for you. The challenging bit is popularizing the website.

You can achieve that through social media platforms or allowing companies to post their ads at subsidized fees. Once the site is popular enough, you can then proceed to reap the full benefits of having companies and individuals post their ads on your website. The details of creating your website are provided in section 2; and popularizing your site in section 3.

4. Try Affiliate Marketing

You have now build your own website and made it attractive enough. It is time to use it in more than one way to earn money. Affiliate marketing is that extra way to make that extra dollar.

Affiliate marketing involves selling other people's products on your website for a commission. You can also promote other websites and brands on your website. Affiliate marketing explores reputable and popular websites to promote newer websites or products. Please read chapter 13 to learn affiliate marketing details.

5. Develop Software And Applications

With the inception of smart phones and tablets, there has been a growing demand for newer and better software. You can make good use of your programming skills to earn decent cash. Strive to develop software that is robust enough to overcome the many challenges faced by existing ones.

Phone applications (apps) also have a very high demand. These include game applications and basic utilities. Take advantage of the many templates and tutorials available online and complement that with your own creativity to produce an application or software that people would want to spend money on.

6. Online Betting

This is yet another fantastic way of making easy money. There are a good number of websites that provide betting opportunities for sporting events. You don't even have to be a sports genius to make use of online betting. It's more or less a matter of luck.

Individuals have also found a better way of exploiting the online betting sites. They have come up with a risk-free scheme called matched betting where they bet against themselves in two different betting sites. This automatically increases your odds of winning. Matched betting is fully legal and tax-free. All you need is an initial investment to bet with.

7. Stock Markets

Stock or exchange markets provide one with the opportunity to earn thousands of dollars within seconds. All you need is knowledge of how the stock markets work. With that, you can monitor the changes online and make the appropriate buys or sells.

Exchanging currencies can also be quite profitable. The exchange rates are constantly fluctuating due to economic, political and social factors. You need to be sharp enough to take advantage of the markets and buy when the prices are low and sell when they are high.

In conclusion, these are just some of the many ways in which you can better utilize your online time. In a world where people are constantly losing jobs and the employment requirements becoming ridiculously many, you can't afford to let such opportunities pass you by.

If you are looking to get into internet marketing, then it is important to know about the basics. Knowing what the basics are can help you get a good start in the internet marketing industry. With that said, below are the four main basics of internet marketing.

1. Website Design Matters

It doesn't matter what type of business you are involved in or what types of products or services you are providing, it is important to have a website that looks great. In other words, you need to have a well-designed website because it can make all the difference in the world, as your website is one of the most powerful assets that you have, at least when it comes to marketing and when it comes to reaching your target market.

You want to make sure that your site is easy to navigate and people can find exactly what they are looking for without having to spend a lot of time searching for it. Not only that, you want to make sure that you have a clear "call to action" on your site. You want to make sure your viewers and visitors know what it is that you want them to do. Also, the content should be fresh and up-to-date. If you are not familiar with website design or development, then it may be worth it to look into hiring a professional web developer, as they will be able to help create a website that suits your needs. Consider advertising your website design project on elance.com to hire a web developer at a reasonable price, even if he/she is in another country.

2. Get Smart With SEO

Search engine optimization (SEO) is something you have probably heard of, but you may not have a full understanding of it. That's ok, because a lot has changed in the SEO world, especially over the course of the last few years. If you don't know what SEO is, it is basically optimizing your site or content for the search engines such as Google, with the goal being to increase the visibility of it in the search engines' results' pages. The better your content and website ranks, the more traffic you will receive, which is what you want when it comes to internet marketing.

With the above said, you should be using smarter SEO techniques, which means that you need to be fully aware of the SEO methods you are using. When it comes to smart SEO techniques, you can try doing thing such as improving your author rank, as well as focusing more on social media sharing and you can also be active on Google+, but don't overdo it with your link building. If you keep these things in mind, then your internet marketing efforts should pay off, but always pay attention to what you are doing in terms of SEO. If you are considering hiring a professional, then make sure you know exactly what they are going to be doing for you. Take the time when looking for an SEO professional to hire, as some are better than others, so use one you feel comfortable with, as well as one that provides quality and smart SEO services.

3. Build An Email List

One of the most important basics of internet marketing is list building, as in building an email list. As a matter of fact, when it comes to internet marketing, having an email list is almost just as important as having a well-designed website. Some businesses and marketers consider having an email list to be the most important tool they have. So, if you plan on getting serious with your internet marketing efforts, then you will want to focus on building an email list that contains opt-in subscribers who are interested in what you are offering.

If you want to build an email list, then you will want to use an auto-responder, as well as have a page on your site that allows people to join your email list. You want to give people a reason to subscribe to your list, so consider offering them something free in exchange for them subscribing to your list. You can offer a free digital product or a free newsletter or even a discount and so forth. It is completely up to you as to what you want to offer them, but the important thing is to offer them something of value. When you do build a list of subscribers, make sure you do not spam them, as this can lead to you losing many subscribers.

4. Use Social Media

One of the basics of internet marketing is using social media, and you need to use it often, as more and more people are on social media sites. This means that if you are not on social media, then you are potentially losing out on getting more customers and more subscribers for your email list. You want to do a few things on social media sites, with one of them being building up your presence. You will also want to get people interested in what you are offering them. The larger your following on social media, the better it is because it increases your chances of becoming a successful internet marketer.

As a rule of thumb, you should join at least 3-5 social media sites. With so many popular sites out there, it is easy to find ones you can join. For example, you can and should join **Facebook**, **Twitter** and **Instagram**, as well as **YouTube** to name just a few. These sites alone have millions upon millions of users, so it is easy to see why you should be using social media if you want to become successful in internet marketing. Next, you want to be active on these sites and provide people with great useful information and then market your services or products. Don't constantly be marketing your products and services. If you do it too often, then you may lose followers. As a rule of thumb, 1 out of every 8-10 posts should be a marketing or promotional post. Please go to section 3 for more details on social media marketing.

The above basics should help you out. Apply them and you could become successful in internet marketing. The sooner you implement these tips, the sooner you can reach your internet marketing goals.

SECTION 2: HOW TO CREATE WEB PRESENCE

Chapter 3: How To Design A Free Website

There are a lot of people who own websites. You can easily join in the fun and maybe make some money too. There are free website making services that will allow you to make a website in a short time and it will be on the web in a very short time too. Here are some few tips of how you can make a free website effectively.

The first thing you do is to find a service. You will have to ask yourself the kind of service you want and it's your needs that will help you choose the best hosting company – the one that meets most of your needs. If you are planning to do business, you have to ensure that the company supports online store services. There are a lot of hosting companies that have specialist in maintaining wikis and blogs.

From there you will have to find a free website builder. There are a lot of them online – some are good, some poor, some expensive and some cheap. You will have to compare them for a while before you decide on which to work with. Most of these companies tend to put a limited services to free websites and they may even put advertisements on your website. You will be a sub-domain of the host site and not your own site.

You will have to compare the services offered because they are being offered free of charge. You should also check on what they limit and see if you can work with it. There are some web hosting companies that will limit the amount of data you can upload to the site – you should avoid such a company.

You need to know if you are planning on a media related website, then you should not go for a free website.

Each hosting company has its own policies on online stores. Check them and decide whether you can work with them. You need also to check if the hosting company will allow you to upload your own website because most of them have their own tools and templates. These are the sites that won't allow you to upload your own custom code. This may cater for most of the basic needs, but if you want more make sure the company allows it.

There are a lot of website themes provided by the hosting company. Go through them and decide on the best theme that can fit your business. These pre-made themes are also called templates or styles. You also have an option of buying these themes from a marketplace websites e.g. Theme Forrest. However, most companies have special designs that help them maintain a brand of their websites.

For free webhosting services, the website might use adverts or at one point you may be asked to upgrade and get some more features. This simply means you will have to pay more for the services. Whichever way you choose, ensure you know how much it might cost you in the future in case you want more features.

The other step is creating the website. You will need to create an account with the web host. There are some companies that will require you add billing options in case you will want to upgrade to a paid account. You need to give them all legal information they require because you never know where the site might become in the future.

Next, you will choose a suitable domain name. Most hosting companies will allow you to create a sub-domain in their host domain and you will not have to pay anything. There are those companies that will allow you to connect your already existing domain to their host domain. There are top-levels domains that you can buy and connect them to the host domain.

There are website design programs that will help you to make your free websites. They will allow you to choose from pre-made themes and give you the freedom to customize it with CSS. These web design programs will help you design your website, add text and images and you will have your website running in no time. There are also tutorials provided by the company that are very useful to a beginner.

From there, you will add valuable content to your website. This is the time to tell your clients what you do or sell. It will do you good if you tell them why you do what you do – this is the story behind your website or business. You should also provide a way for them to contact you. With time you should create new content to ensure you stay relevant in the market.

When you are satisfied with the website layout and content, it is the time to publish and start business. If you are running a blog, you should have an introduction space where you can do your announcements and also introduce yourself and what you do. This is a way of making your readers feel welcomed and they will have the interest to read on and know more about you and your website.

You should not let your website be dormant. Keep updating new content as it will help you grow and remain relevant to your site visitors and clients. Create engaging content that will bring the visitors back for more. Come up with an update schedule that you will stick to and your readers will get used to it. The only way you will have more readers is to create good and relevant topics that the readers can relate to their needs.

There are ways you can generate some income using your website. You can do this through creating advertisements. However, you will have to check if your web hosting company allows it. Most of the host companies do not allow free hosts to earn ad revenue. You should be careful not to chase people away with too much adverts.

If you wish to get a website hosted, you may think that you can't do this because you don't know where to start among so many options. That's why you'll find this chapter to be helpful to you. There are going to be quite a few pieces of advice here and that way you can go from not knowing much about hosting to knowing enough to get your website up online. It's best to think through this carefully or else you may not have your website doing too well online causing it to be a waste of time and money.

The first order of business is to find out what the main hosting companies are. They can be reached out to if need be so you can learn what they have to offer. Figure out what their pricing structure is like, how much they can offer in the way of features, and how often their servers go down to have maintenance done on them. A website for a host should have the features listed, but know that sometimes they add more or take away features so that information may not be what is still true.

A good web hosting company will have deals for those that are doing a new sign up. If you just look around and keep looking, you should be able to find a hosting company that's having a sale of some kind to attract new people into their service. If you can't find anything on their site, do a quick search on a search engine for the name of the host and promo codes. You can then usually get a good percentage off of what you order and that way you can get more hosting and time for a lot less.

It is a lot of work to set up a website if you don't have the right hosting tools. Usually you get a control panel when you work with a host, and from there you are able to upload files or even use a built in plugin that installs Wordpress or other content management systems for you. The main thing you have to keep in mind is that when you are working with a host's software, it's a matter of going through the help they offer and then asking the support team questions if you still don't understand what to do.

A lot of the hosting services you can get are going to be cheap at first, and then the price will go up later on. Look very closely at the terms when signing up, because you do not want to be surprised by them at a later date. The sign up deal you take advantage of should be analyzed so you can determine if after the initial low price is up the service is still priced in a way that makes it fair for you to use. Otherwise, you could get stuck with a hosting package you're responsible for paying that's too high when compared to all other services.

The customer service that a host has to offer is important, especially when you first get into using this kind of service. They need to have a way for you to get in touch with someone quickly. Otherwise, if you have a website issue you may lose a lot of traffic and it will cause your website not to be worth what you are paying. Try contacting a host's customer service with a simple question before signing up just to see how fast they respond.

The host will have to have a lot of up time or else it will mean that your website can lose visitors. When you have a website that is having issues that cause it to go down, people aren't going to be able to see it and you won't even be able to really put a message onto it about what's going on. If you notice your website is down, contact the hosting company right away. Figure out when it will be back up and if you have followers on social media or anywhere you can reach them then you can let them know what's happening.

When looking into a host, make sure you know what you're allowed to put onto their servers. They probably won't let you, for instance, host anything illegal. You may also find some hosts that will not allow for you to place anything that has a copyright onto your page. The hosts are all different in what they allow, so if you have adult content or anything you're not sure about, it's best to ask them to let you know what you can and cannot be putting onto their servers.

Backups are important, and you need to have them done on a regular basis. There may be a service that your host provides that does this for you. Even if that's the case, try to get all of your website's files downloaded into a backup folder. Then place this folder online in the cloud so you have access to it no matter what. The worst thing that could happen is your site gets damaged, and the host also lost your backup on their end. So if you have your files saved away at your own, you can be back in business without too much of an issue.

Once you are familiar with how to get a website hosted, you can then get it online and have people start to visit. The better the host, the more of a chance you have to get a lot of great traffic. Hosts that go down all the time or those that don't offer a lot of good features may just make your website frustrating to deal with and it won't last you very long. Now that you are better equipped to deal with getting a good host, you can get started and share your website with the world soon!

Doing search engine optimization (SEO) sounds difficult especially if you are new to this field'. However, it is a must learn thing if you want to improve your sites interaction with the search engines and the users. This chapter focuses on some of the things you must do to optimize the search engine.

First and foremost, it is important to understand that search engine optimization is about modifying parts of your website , improving it so that it can have a noticeable impact on the user experience and performance in organic search results by internet search engines such as Google. The best optimization decision is based on what is good to the consumer of the content. Second it must be search engine friendly since web surfers use the search engine to access your work. Remember, SEO is all about putting your sites best foot forward so that it is visible to the search engine.

Below are some essential SEO steps and tips:

1. Creating Unique Page Titles

The first thing you must do towards optimization is to create unique and accurate page title tags. The most important titles you must consider include: The title of the home page. If the users perform a search, your home page should be able to show up. The title should thus have the services that you offer as a key word. The title tag tells the user and the search engine about the content of the page. This is why it is important to create a different and unique title for each page.

2. Make use of the description Meta tag

The description Meta tag gives an overview of what the site engages in. A page description Meta tags gives Google a summary of what your page is all about. The difference between a pages title and a description Meta tag is that the latter may be a short paragraph or just a few sentences. You can tell whether your description Meta tags are too short or too long by using Google Webmaster tools to analyze the section. Google may opt to use the description Meta tags to snippets your pages or it may choose to use the sites description. Adding description Meta to each of the pages is thus a good idea that can help improve on the snippet.

Ensure that you:

- Summarize the content of the page
- Use generic description such as "this page is about soccer"
- Copy and paste the entire content of the document into the description Meta tags

Things to avoid

- A description that can disinterest the user
- Using a similar description across all the pages of the site

3. Make use of images

Ensure that you provide image for the content wherever possible. You may store files in the directories which are managed using common file formats. Consolidating the images in a single directory is better.

4. Making use of robots.txt

Robot txt can be used to restrict the crawlers where they are not needed. Ensure that you manage your information and keep a grasp on any information you do not want to be crawled. The file that tells the search engine whether they can access and crawl on the site must be named as a robot txt and placed in the root directory of the site.

5. Making The Site Mobile Friendly

Ensure that your site is mobile friendly. This is important because it ensures that the site can be accessed on mobile devices, such as, smart phones and tablets. If this is not the case, you need to set up a mobile friendly site all together and verify that it is indexed by Google. You need to redirect the mobile users to the mobile friendly website. But you must ensure that your site's content is similar, if not exactly the same, whether accessed from a desk top or a mobile device.

6. Make The Site Easier To Navigate

A site that is easier to navigate and find what you are looking for is not just important to the visitor but to the search engine as well. Google prefer having a sense of the importance and relevance of the page to the entire site. Thus, if your page has more than one page, it is important to organize it so that the visitors can easily find the information they may be looking for.

To visitors, the navigation of a website is extremely important as it helps them to find the content they are looking for quickly. Besides, it can be helpful to search engines as it enables the search engines to recognize the content that webmaster considers as important. Google as well prefers to have a sense of the role played by a page in the broader picture of the site.

All sites have home page, which is also referred to as root page. For most visitors this is the starting place of navigation page that they most frequent on the site. You need to think of how visitors will navigate from your home page to a page with more specific content.

You should ensure that you have adequate pages around a particular topic area so that it would be logical to create a page that describes the pages that are related to it and those that are similar.

7. Improve the Structure of Your URLs

Even though Google is good at crawling all sorts of URL structures, it is important to make your URLs as simple as possible. This will be helpful for users as well as search engines. There are several webmasters who attempt to achieve this by rewriting their active URLs to static ones. However, this is an advanced procedure that could cause crawling problems if done wrongly. On the other hand, Google has no problem with this procedure. URLs that are easily understood will convey content information without any difficulties. URLs are normally shown in search results.

8. Optimizing Content

You should create descriptive categories as well as filenames for the documents on your website. Apart from helping you to keep your site better organized, it might also result into better crawling of your documents by search engines. Visitors may find very long and cryptic URLs containing few recognizable words intimidating.

Chapter 6: How To Generate Free and Paid Traffic For Your Website

As a business person, all you want is to sell as many products as possible. To achieve this, you will need to reach out to as many prospective clients as you can and here is where internet marketing comes in. The online platform has, over the past few years, proved to be one of the most efficient and effective marketing tools. The problem is that the numbers do not just come with no efforts. You need to create a website and find multiple ways to get traffic to it.

As far as generating traffic is concerned, it is a tough process. You need to make sure that you have good content on your site and that the site is specific enough so that you do not end up attracting just any traffic, but you attract the relevant potential customers. Below are some ways to create relevant traffic for your website or blog. Remember there are ways to generate traffic for free, but in some cases you will need to pay for it.

1. Advertise your website

Well, to get customers to know your product through any media, the first thing to do always is advertise. You can do this on social media that can be free or paid. As for the free advertising, it means you will need to create a page on social media and invite people to follow, subscribe or like. Also, you will be posting updates of new products and pictures as well.

Alternatively, Google or Facebook for instance can do it for you if you want to advertise there. There you will have to pay for their pay-per-click (PPC) program and your ads will appear on the side bar. When Google or Facebook visitors click on your ad, your credit card gets charged based on the money amount you have set up for each click. You do have an option of allocating a set budget to spend each day. After that pre-defined quota is reached, your ads are not displayed until next day. Make sure your advertising strategies are in tandem with the ultimate goals you aim to achieve. Paying for traffic PPC ads can be very expensive, so it is prudent that you assess your marketing goals before setting up a PPC campaign.

2. Use catchy headlines

Content is the king. No matter how much you advertise, if you do not have good content on your website, you won't get people stay longer and re-visit your site. What you got to do is to ensure that you have great content starting with catchy headlines. The risky thing with catchy titles is that you may end up attracting the wrong audience. So you need to be careful and tune your titles to attract the targeted traffic within your niche. For example, you do not want people interested in losing weight visiting your "dog training" website, and vice-versa. It is quite frustrating for web surfers looking for relevant information, and also waste of your marketing money and efforts.

Remember, you can have great products and a great blog, but without a compelling headline, odds of great traffic turnaround are against you. You can apply the rule of ten, where you write down ten possible titles before settling for one. This makes the process thorough and you get to have the best headlines.

3. Optimize your content for Search Engines

Many people think search engine optimization (SEO) is a cliché thing, but the truth is SEO is still here with us in this day and age. Optimizing your content is a worthwhile thing to do so that search engines can pick your website first. Utilize meta descriptions, create internal links, make as much as you can out of image alt text. Optimizing your content will get as much organic content to your site as you possibly can. The details of SEO have been discussed previously in chapter 5.

4. Long tail keywords

Making the most of keywords is one of the most effective ways to getting traffic to your website. Long-tail keywords are keywords that make up most of the web searches. This means if SEO or paid searches (PPC) mean anything to you, long-tail keywords are the first thing to include on your website.

5. Guest blog

Guest blogging is another cliché activity that can generate traffic for your website. Securing a guest post on a popular site can get you crazy traffic. It will also make your brand believable, especially if it is displayed on a respected brand site. Be careful though because there have been new regulations for guest blogging. Guest blogging works but do it cautiously. Invite others to your site by commenting on it and leaving your links on theirs. Guest blogging goes both ways, read other people's blogs and they'll read yours.

6. Have videos in your content

Having videos in your website content is definitely of great benefit. Text is great, but the video is greater. It makes your site more interactive and inviting. Visual materials can be remembered for a long time. Whether it is still pictures or motion, all that matters is getting visuals.

7. Research about your competitors

Use software like BuzzSumo to get information about the work of your competitors. This software gives you an idea of what exactly others are doing and the topics readers are looking forward to at that particular moment, and also those trending on social media. Write similar real time topics and trends and strive to get your site visitors involved with relevant and useful information.

8. Attend groupings that talk about what you do

Attend conferences, meetings, exhibitions, conventions or whatever groupings that will be discussing what you are doing. It is important to find your footing in the industry.

9. Make sure your site can load quickly

A site that does not load quickly will get your visitors' attention diverted. It is quite a bit of work to get your website visitors and retain them. You should have it clear in your mind: online visitors are impatient. Consider hiring a web designer to optimize your website pages for the best results. Let he or she advise you on matters like how big your images should be, how to structure your pages, concerns such as third party plugins and so on. If your website can load faster, better it is for you and your business.

There isn't one single specific way to get traffic to your website or blog. For this reason, take advantage of every possible promotion area that is available to you. As for your content, make it as diverse as possible. Use different lengths, formats and so on, so that it becomes appealing to your readers' eyes and minds.

SECTION 3: HOW TO DO SOCIAL MEDIA MARKETING FOR FREE TRAFFIC

Chapter 7: How To Do Facebook Marketing For Your Website

Having a website is one of the first steps that you need to take to run a successful online business. After you have spent time developing the website and turning it into something that will look impressive to the visitors, it is then time to start using social media for marketing your website. You could have one of the best looking sites to have ever existed, but you will not have a lot of people visiting it if you are not marketing for it.

If you want to start marketing on Facebook, the first step involves creating a business account. Avoid using your personal account, even if the website belongs solely to you. It is crucial to keep business separate from the personal connections you have with your friends.

After making the account, you will need to upload a profile picture and a cover photo that both represent your business by matching the style of your website.

Once you have the page, it is time to start getting followers. Instead of buying them, try gaining followers in a natural way.

You can start by asking customers who have already purchased your products or services to like your page in exchange for a 10% discount on their next purchase or for a free item with their next purchase. Offering an incentive will improve your chances of getting more likes.

After you have started to gain these followers, start throwing contests. Offer a prize to a random follower for a specific amount that fits within your budget once you reach a certain amount of likes.

You could also offer to give the person who gets the most people to like your page a prize. The people who like your page would need to let you know who it is that sent them on over.

It may seem like a lot of work, but it is actually simple and worth it. If someone wants to receive a free product, a cash prize or something else of that nature, they are going to tell as many people as they know about your page, which will result in a lot more followers. Having natural followers who are interested in what your website entails will help you get more traffic flowing on your website, thus resulting in more exposure.

Although Facebook is a great way to get more exposure via word-of-mouth, you will need to log into your account each day and continue posting useful content as often as possible.

Create engaging, interesting and useful posts that people will want to discuss and comment on. Get involved in the conversation with customers and those who could become customers of yours in the future.

When you run an active Facebook page with lots of intriguing posts, you will be able to start getting more likes and keep them interested in checking out your page. Some people may log into their accounts with the sole purpose of visiting your page to see what you have posted for the day.

They may want to see whether or not you are offering any special deals for products on your website. If you can keep up with this form of marketing, you can do well, even if it takes a bit to build it up.

Twitter is a short message communication tool by which you can send out tweets (messages) up to 140 characters long to your followers (people who subscribe to you). Your tweets may include a link to a blog post, website page, PDF document, or any other web content, or a photograph or video

By having people follow (subscribe to) your account and you following other people, you can read, reply and conveniently re-tweet (share their tweets with your followers).

Twitter is unique in the sense that a tweet is like a short Facebook status. In addition, unlike the filter of Facebook's EdgeRank, every tweet arrives at every follower's feed. Twitter allows you to follow anyone, even strangers, which is very helpful in targeting potential customers for your website.

A tweet is similar to a short Google+ status update. Twitter lets you organize people into categories that organize conversations similar to Google+ groups.

The following guidelines can be helpful in Twitter marketing for your website.

1. To begin with, ensure that you pin a tweet on the top of your profile because it will remain at the top of your Twitter profile page. Besides, it will be the initial tweet that will be seen when people visit your profile.

2. In case you use a free product to lure people into signing up for your mailing list, ensure that you tweet it out frequently.

3. Develop Relationships. Engagement is crucial to twitter social marketing. However, engaging with small influencers is simply not enough. The best way to use this tool is to establish relationships with Twitter influencers – that is, people who have numerous followers, who tweet frequently, and are very active on the social network. By connecting with these influencers, sharing their tweets, replying back to their tweets and engaging with their content (even if it is on a different social media platform), you will be able to market your business successfully on Twitter. This will make you catch their eye and discover that you are one of their champions. As a result, they will be eager to get to know you better.

4. Avoid using a Twitter validation system since this is an additional step that will need people to follow you. In most cases, people will just avoid this step and it can potentially lose you followers.

5. Utilize Twitter chats. Twitter chats work with hash tags which can be likened to a lifeline on Twitter. They actually work best for locating active Twitter friends who will increase your interactions. They are useful for generating quality content for your blogs and also surveying people about a specific industry trend. Hash tags should be used strategically, and as such should not be overused.

Your content must add value to the Twitter users. You are the one who understands your audience best enough to give them content that brings value to them in a way that is linked to your business. Many people perceive content as beneficial if it is in a specific how-to style. It builds the impression that you are an expert and someone who can be relied on to provide valuable advice in your industry. This may result into business for you.

Chapter 9: How To Start Marketing Your Website On Instagram

You understand that social media marketing is important, especially if you want to have lots of visitors on your website. Now that you have created an Instagram page, you may not know exactly how to get started. Before you start attempting to get followers and following other people on this social media site, you need to add a picture that best describes your website.

The main picture that you use does not have to include the name of your website, especially if it is already mentioned on your page. Instead, you could use a picture of one of the items that you sell or a picture that you have taken that relates to the content that is on your website. For example, if your website is all about fitness and helping people become healthy, the picture could relate to that niche in some way.

Add a new photo each day of something, whether it is an inspirational quote, a useful product that people who like your website may find useful or something else of that nature. Because Instagram is all about uploading pictures, you should make sure to use some hash tags in the description. Those who use the search feature on this social media site may be able to find your page based on the types of hash tags you choose to use.

You can target people using hash tags. Not only can they find your Instagram page, but you can find theirs too. You may want to target an audience based on what your website entails. It may be geared toward people of certain ages or health enthusiasts.

If you were targeting college students, for example, you could always search for hash tags that may indicate the person is in college, such as #collegelife or #dormlife. It is an easy way for you to find the people you may want to start following. After you follow them, they will likely return the favor.

Many website owners hold special contents to gain more followers. There are some people who love a product, service or even a website so much that they will tell their friends right away without receiving anything for it. However, most people are a bit more motivated to spread the word about things if they know that there is a chance for them to win something, so why not give it a try too?

Brainstorm ideas for contests that go along with the type of website that you have. If you do run a fitness website, you may want to do a giveaway of assorted exercise and fitness gear, such as a reusable water bottle, running sneakers and a gym bag. If you are creative, you will have a better chance of catching the attention of people on Instagram.

You can even market for your website by leaving comments on the pictures of other people. You definitely do not want to spam them, but you can leave a compliment on their photo, along with a suggestion to follow your page or visit your website. You will have to dedicate at least an hour or two on marketing alone each day if you want it to work for you. This time period does not have to be in one stretch, and can be applied throughout the day whenever you have time from your other activities or when you want a break from your routine work.

There are a few good reasons why YouTube should be part of any marketing plan. The main reason is that video is the latest trend in the digital world, with many people preferring to watch a video instead of reading eBooks. Video tutorials are also in high demand, as they are easier to follow than written instructions.

Since everybody is on YouTube, you should be there as well if you want to enjoy a better exposure, higher traffic and more conversions. Moreover, since YouTube belongs to Google, videos on the network are indexed and displayed in Google's SERPs. By marketing your products or services on YouTube, you increase the chances of ranking for various keywords, thus generating a certain amount of additional organic traffic.

If you want to be on YouTube, the first step is to create a channel for your business or brand. This channel allows you to upload videos, receive comments and interact with your followers. Creating a channel is free and there are multiple personalization options, so you can add your branding to it. This is actually the second step after creating your channel. You need to personalize it with a cover and a profile image. Make them relevant and don't forget to add your logo, should you have one.

The next step is the production of video materials. You can record yourself talking with the help of a webcam, so you don't need to spend a lot of money on expensive video recording equipment. If you want, you can record product demos and presentations, so that your visitors understand what your products are about and what you can do to help your customers solve their problems.

If you don't know how to record and edit videos, you can simply use images and create slideshows with music and captions. You can upload such slideshows on YouTube without problems. If you don't have music, you can choose from the options provided by YouTube. All these tunes are free of charge and available to use without any copyright restrictions. They can be helpful especially if you are relatively new in business and you don't have a big marketing budget.

It is very important to tag your videos with the most relevant keywords. YouTube shows related videos for each movie on their network, so you stand good chances to get lots of views from people who watched high traffic videos and clicked on yours in the "related" section. Titles are also important, so make sure you use only relevant ones. The description of the videos should be as detailed as possible. This gives search engines more clues regarding the industry you're in and the topics of your videos. Don't forget to include a link to your website and some contact details, so that users can get in touch with you if needed.

Last but not least, always moderate and reply to comments on your YouTube channel. Maintain an active presence and your followers will like you and will probably become your clients.

SECTION 4: INTERNET MARKETING STRATEGIES

Chapter 11: How To Do Email Marketing

Email marketing is one of the best forms of marketing that you could incorporate into your online strategy. The truth is that email marketing is also one of the most effective strategies for obtaining new customers and retaining them. This is largely due to the amount of people that now have access to the Internet on a regular basis. Because smart phones have become more prominent, an increasing number of people have access to email even while on the go. This means that you have a chance to connect with your customers while they are out and about.

In this chapter, we will be discussing some of the tips to incorporate email marketing into your business.

1. Make It Easy To Subscribe

The first thing that you are going to want to do is make sure that it is very easy to subscribe to your list. You can do this by posting a sign up form on your home page of your website. You could also post it on your Facebook and other social media pages. Simply post your sign up box wherever your fans are already active. This will ensure that everyone that would sign up for your email list, does sign up. You might also want to collect names and birthdays in order to be able to market to your customers on their birthdays.

2. Tell Subscribers What They Should Expect

It is important to tell your subscribers what they should be expecting from signing up to your list. Whether you plan on sending company updates, lettings from the administration, daily deals, or weekly tips, it is very important to let your readers know what they can expect from you. By giving them as much information as possible, you are going to be able to keep your prospective and current customers as happy as possible. If you tell your readers that you are going to be sending them exclusive offers and coupons, be sure to actually send them exclusive offers and coupons.

3. Send a Welcome Email

This is where a lot of email marketers mess up. The fact is getting someone to sign up is difficult. Do not make all of the hard work for nothing by not welcoming your new sign ups to your email list. It is always a good idea to remind the people that they signed up for your list, why they signed up, and reassure them that you will be sending them a lot of good stuff in the near future. You can even try to send your new sign ups special offers and/or exclusive content as a way of thanking them for signing up for your list.

4. Make It Easy To Read

A lot of your subscribers are going to be living extremely busy lives and there In-Boxes are likely already full of a lot of junk emails. Be sure that you are not contributing to junking up their email boxes. Be sure to send them excellent content and/or offers and make your emails extremely easy to recognize and to read/scan. Be sure that they can simply and easily look through your emails and figure out what you are saying and/or offering without having to put too much effort into it.

5. Send Content They Want

It is also important to send your subscribers the content that they actually want. Be sure to segment your email lists if your businesses reaches a broad amount of people. For example, if you have subscribers that signed up to receive information about a specific product, try to segment them to a specific list and away from the subscribers that are subscribed for information about another/different product. This way, you are not going to be bothering your subscribers with things that they simply do not care about.

6. Keep A Publishing Calendar

Do not get stuck not knowing what to post. If you are planning on sending out emails to your subscribers, try to set up a publishing calendar which will allow you to know exactly what you are going to post and when you are going to post it. This will allow you to organize your emails effectively.

7. Think About Mobile

Because of the increasing amount of people that are using their mobile phones to check their emails, it is important that you think about mobile when you are creating your email campaigns. It is important to ensure that your campaigns show up effectively on mobile devices. If they do not, your campaign is bound to fail. Everything you send should be mobile friendly. This will ensure that those use their mobile phones frequently in order to view their emails and other content will be able to see your email effectively without problems. The fact is, around 63% of Americans actually delete their emails that are not properly optimized for mobile viewing.

8. Know Your Spam Rules

Another thing that you are going to want and need to do is to be aware of and follow your spam rules. You should be reading up on the CAN-SPAM act in order to avoid getting into any legal trouble. To put it simply, you are allowed to send bulk email only to people that have specifically told you and given you permission to put them onto your email list. Therefore, if you collected information for a giveaway or to supply event information, you cannot send marketing emails unless you made it clear at the sign up of the email list that you were going to be doing so. You also have to include a very obvious and easy to use unsubscribe link somewhere inside of your emails that can let your subscribes know they can unsubscribe if they want to. you will also want to remind your subscribers how they got onto your email list in the first place so they do not assume you are spamming.

As you can see, there are plenty of tips that you can utilize in order to effectively set up an email marketing campaign. Be sure to follow the tips we have discussed in this chapter.

The internet and the websites that populate it are run on relevant content that describes what a consumer would want to know about a specific topic or subject. When people type a request into a search engine's search box, they are expecting information back when they hit the button that is going to tell them all about what they are looking for.

Article marketing is the creation of articles, at the length of 300 to 500 words that deliver content about a specific subject. Once they are created, they can be submitted to article directories and they will be grouped in specific categories according to the ones that are chosen by the author.

Now the big question is how does article marketing help? The primary purpose of article writing, as far as the author is concerned, is to place a back link or two in the author's box at the end of the article that points back to author's website page that has similar information.

The premise of this procedure is to generate interest in author's website and the content that is contained on the website specifically. It also is used to establish the credibility of the particular author as an expert in the field in which he or she is writing in relation to the content of the website.

The back links to the website will also help to boost the rankings of the website itself in search engines like Google. If enough articles are written, then the better the rankings are perhaps going to be. Another advantage of article marketing is that it is not difficult to do, and it does not cost a fee or any money to accomplish.

Once articles are written, and accepted by the article directory company, they are stored on their website. They can be used by other authors as a means of authority about a certain topic or subject, as long as credit is given to the original author, and the back link to the website is also shown. This gives additional credit and power to the original author, the article, and the back links give more credibility to the website.

It is important to identify you niche, or area of expertise in which you are writing your articles and identifying yourself as an authority. The more articles you write in that area or in that niche, the more authority you will perceive. If the numbers of articles continue to increase, the content about which you have written will continue to be distributed all over the internet, which will improve the visibility and back link authority to your original website.

The titles of your articles are very important because they will identify what niche you are in and what the topic or subject of your article is all about. For each article that you write, your article should be slightly different, but still on topic in the same subject area. In this way, all of your articles will be grouped together in the same niche, or subject area, all giving a wave of credibility to you and your expertise in the subject matter.

Keep your titles short, and keep them as concise as you possibly can. The title of an article should reflect as closely as possible on what the subject matter is all about. Stay away from the temptation of trying to come up with a catchy title just to get attention. You want your article title to say exactly what the subject matter of the article is going to say.

Do a very thorough search for relevant keywords. Keywords are the words or phrases that people are going to use to type into the search box of the search engine. First of all, find out what the keywords or phrases are going to be, and then build your article around those keywords or phrases.

Be sure to put two to three keywords or phrases in about every 500 to 600 words of the article. In a 500 word article, put 2 keywords in the top half of the article, and only one in the bottom half, near the end of the article.

Be sure that your article contains unique content and is of superior quality, as that's the only type of writing that people will want to read. Make it informative, describe how products look, how they perform, how people like them and so forth.

Take the time to organize your articles by having an opening paragraph, a body of the article, and then finish with a closing paragraph. A good rule of thumb to follow is to have your article have one paragraph for each main idea that gives support to the opening statement of your article. Each paragraph should then have three to five sentences. If you have short and explanatory sentences in the paragraphs, they are more readable to people, than if the paragraphs that are longer.

Most article companies will allow you to place links back to your website, and in many cases they have a special author's box located at the end of the article. Here you can tell a little about yourself, as well as a summary of what you just wrote. It is here that many article companies will allow you to put a hyperlink back to your website.

If you have a blog, a newsletter, or if you are active on social media, all of these venues can, and should, be used to promote your articles. This gives the articles more importance as well as having them relate to your website in a more focused manner.

One tactic that generates interest in an article is to feature it on a blog or a newsletter, and only publish part of the first paragraph, with a link that states "more", or "Read More," and then have the rest of the article continue on your website. That gets more readers to your site.

Article marketing can be a very valuable way to increase interest in your website, and it should be one of the main factors in the quest for improving the rankings of your website.

Affiliate marketing is a kind of referral marketing where a business rewards people (affiliates) for every customer or visitor they bring to them through their own marketing efforts. Affiliate marketing industry has four core gamer players: (1) the business entity (also called 'retailer' or 'brand'), (2) the network (consisting of the offers for the affiliates to select from as well as means to get their commissions), (3) the writer (also called 'the affiliate'), and (4) the customers.

Affiliate marketing overlaps with other online marketing techniques to a great extent, because affiliate marketers frequently use internet for their marketing efforts. These online marketing techniques include organic Search Engine Optimization (SEO), Pay Per Click (PPC) or Pay Per View (PPV) campaigns, e-mail marketing, content marketing, and banner advertising. Sometimes affiliate marketers use review article techniques, such as, posting reviews of products or services on their blogs that are offered by the business they are affiliated with.

Followings are the proven steps to be successful with the highly lucrative affiliate marketing industry:

1. Realize That Success Is A Process

If you Google or YouTube "Affiliate Marketing" you will find no shortage of self-proclaimed gurus who promise that they can take you from novice to super affiliate overnight. Unfortunately, this is a far cry from the truth. What you must immediately realize is that affiliate marketing is a skill and it takes time to develop. Even after you have the basics down, success will not immediately happen. The form of marketing you choose will also play a factor in how long it takes before you start to see success. The best approach is to learn affiliate marketing as a process. This is something you will need to work hard at, something that may hand you a ton of failures, and if you stick with it something that will hand you your share of success. Affiliate marketing is not like showing up to a job and just receiving a paycheck for the hours you put in. Instead, it rewards the bold, the relentless, the creative and those who never give up. You will learn from your failures, and those first lessons will make you decide what an effective marketing strategy is and what isn't. If this excites you, if you know that you have to learn affiliate marketing, if you are willing to do the work, then you will find success.

2. Figure Out Your Bread-n-Butter Marketing Strategy

Affiliate marketing is not a style of marketing but more an explanation of the relationship that a marketer has with their product. With affiliate marketing you are promoting someone else's product and not your own. The main benefit of this is that you don't have to invest any time, money or effort into R&D. You also will know if a product is successful or not before you market it and this information is typically provided by affiliate networks who will provide conversion stats on each affiliate product.

When it comes to the actual marketing of affiliate products, you have many options. The most popular methods of marketing are SEO, PPC, video marketing, e-mail marketing and social media. Each one of these have their own benefits, their own pros and cons, and their own learning curve. PPC requires that you have start up cash to implement but the result (good or bad) are almost immediate. SEO (search engine optimization) is all about creating websites and performing techniques that will make Google and other search engines display your website link on the first page of keyword searches that relate to your website. SEO (chapter 5) can take weeks to several months to be successful but it is worth the wait. Social media (section 3) is obvious and deals more with building rapport with followers, it is typically free and is easy to get started with. You can also do PPC on social media and many marketers are finding a lot of success with this model. Some recommend that it is the best form of PPC for new marketers. Video marketing is great and YouTube (chapter 10) has a lot of traffic and is the second leading search engine behind Google. People love seeing videos and if you can provide solution to their problems, they will do business with you. E-mail marketing (chapter 11) can be an offshoot of all these other methods and you can collect e-mails from traffic that comes from each of these other forms of marketing. With e-mail marketing you can send list members important and valuable information about your products and build a rapport with them over time.

3. Find Affiliate Products To Market

The next step is to actually find affiliate product to market. The best way to do this is to Google affiliate networks, create a list of a few and then try to find the reputation of each affiliate network. The most important thing is to figure out if they make on time payments and if they are easy to work with or not. You can also sign up for multiple affiliate networks and this will give you access to many different affiliate products.

4. Have A Marketing Plan And Work Your Plan

Choose the way or ways in which you plan to market affiliate products and put your plan into action. It is intelligent to use multiple marketing strategies and to stay consistent with your actions. Ultimately you will need to create a process to quickly implement your marketing program. Right after you read this chapter go ahead and start formulating a marketing plan that you will immediately put into action. Take steps, create an outline, a to-do list and incrementally work through your list.

5. Expand Your Marketing Techniques And Stay In The Game

Always add to your knowledge base. Over the last decade many marketing strategies that once worked and that once earned marketers a lot of money have been destroyed. Marketers who didn't diversify their efforts, who didn't continue to learn, who put all their eggs into one basket--- were all hit hard with some of them having to leave the business. The smart ones who continued to learn and try new things are still up and running.

What this ultimately means is that you need to market a product in many different ways. You need to do SEO, social media, video marketing, e-mail marketing and even PPC. The goal is that if one method stops working, you have the other ones. Besides the fear of one method failing, diversifying your efforts also allows you to reach more people.

Conclusion: Put these ideas into action

It is now time to put the ideas above into action. This isn't a chapter for your entertainment or even "infotainment" but instead these are all ideas that you need to immediately jump on. One thing that separates those who end up making a lot of money and those who never do is their ability to hit the floor running. Get started today and keep going until you are successful.

Mobile marketing is one of the best ways for business owners to be able to effectively market their products and/or services in today's marketplace. The reason why mobile marketing is so effective as a lead generation and sales generation tool is because virtually everyone has access to mobile devices nowadays. Also, because of the widespread and increasing adoption rate of smart phones and tablets, an increasing number of people now have access to the Internet on the go.

In this chapter, we will be going over some of the best tips to implement mobile marketing into your business.

1. Opt In

The first step to get mobile marketing set up for your business is to get customers and prospective customers to opt into your mobile marketing list. Your mission is to get people to opt in to your list in order to be able to market to them in the future. The best way to get people to opt into your list is to ask them at the point of sale. At this point, the customer has already decided that they like your products and/or services. Therefore, you should be able to generate a good amount of opt-ins by asking at the point of sale. If you are trying to get prospective customers to opt in to your mobile marketing list, you can do so by sending out advertising flyers marketing your opt in list.

2. Offers

The next thing that you are going to need to do is to come up with a strategy that you are going to be able to effectively implement and utilize in your business. Ideally, you are going to want to come up with different offers that you can use in order to entice people to come into your business and also get retained as regular customers in the long run. The key to coming up with offers is to think of things that are low cost for your business that you can give away that still have a good amount of value. For instance, if you are a fast food restaurant, you might decide that you can give away a free burger to anyone that signs up for your mobile marketing opt in list. The reason why is because you know that one burger doesn't cost much especially when you consider the fact that they are giving you contact information which will allow you to market to them in the future to generate more business from it. If you do not come up with attractive offers, your marketing campaigns will simply fall flat and they will not increase the amount of traffic and/or business for you.

3. No Spamming

It is critical that you respect your mobile list. Let them know how many times they can expect you to send out a mobile offer and/or text message. Be sure that you do not spam them and annoy them. Limit the amount of times you send out text messages to around one per week or even once every two weeks. This will keep your list happy and keep your mobile marketing effective.

SECTION 5: BLOGGING AND WORDPRESS

Chapter 15: How Blogging Can Make You Money

There are more and more people who have taken up blogging as a means of making extra money online. The purpose could be only to earn a few extra dollars as supplemental income, or it could be set as a goal to replace a full time income from a job or an occupation.

Some bloggers are in college working towards their tuition, and some are retired people who want to supplement their income. There are currently tens of thousands of people who do make money from blogging.

So what is a blog? The word "blog" comes from the term that was called "web logging". So when you combine these two words together, you get the word "blog."

In order to set the stage about what you can expect and how you should go about getting involved with blogging, we need to understand a few things. First of all, not everyone gets filthy rich by blogging, although some do make a pile of money. It is possible to earn an income from your blogging efforts, but it takes lots of hard work and persistency.

Each blog is unique and will fall on different ears all of the time. Some blogs are written about huge interests that are wildly popular, while others are niche blogs that cover very narrow topics.

The first rule of blogging is that you must write about something that you are passionate about, because you need to convey that passion to your readers. A good blogger will be able to write and write, in great depth, as well as having an effect on the readers in a positive way.

The blogger will also need to be able to answer questions that come up from readers, or deal with opinions that are expressed along the way too. Sometimes people have difficulty in discovering what they are passionate about, or they just feel that their passion is not one which anyone else might have - what can be done about that?

Do some more research, and find out what other people are concerned about. If you do enough study you will be able to pick out a need that you can get involved with too, and one with which you can become passionate.

People are most concerned about things that affect their lives, both positive and negative. They are truly looking for answers, so in effect, you can become a clearing house for solutions to the problems of others. That may sound too simplistic, but most people never spend any time looking for solutions on their own, and that is where you come in.

People are interested in hobbies too, such as quilting, cooking out, golfing, hiking, pets, gardening, and hundreds of other topics that you can research and with which you can get involved.

As far as the mechanics of blogging, there are hundreds of good tutorials on the internet, some for pay and some for free. Just be sure that you learn from someone who is already at it and successful. Most of the money that comes in from blogging is from running ads on the blog, just like the magazines do. If you learn to do that right, people will thank you for running the ads, as it will be a help to them in their daily living experiences.

To be a successful blogger, you have to be an innovator, and be able to see problems solved before they really become critical. The problems themselves can be quite evident, but you need to deal with problems that can be solved in a number of different ways.

Things such as child behavior, growing a good garden, canning, etc, are largely problems about organization. Some people are willing to pay money for an e-book on the subject. Many people are just terrible at organizing things, and sometimes a little push in the right direction can be a big help.

The creation of your own products is another way to make money. Many successful bloggers have spent years building up their list of followers, and they have wooed them and catered to their needs for a long time. In this way, a blogger has a following who trusts what is said on the blog. It is simply there, and it works, so people like to stick with what they know.

If you come up with an idea to make flowers grow better by using average household goods for plant food, and you package this in a special way, you will probably be able to sell it on your blog. One lady and her husband came up with specially made dog food that is nutritious to beat the band, and they sell it all over. No matter that it is cooked at home on their stove, the dogs love it and a great following has been created.

Blogs are simply communicating with people, but an even more important phrase is resonating. People want to buy into the blog philosophy, so they are ready for fresh and good ideas on how to do stuff. They like the interaction that a blog gives them, as the ability to respond to the blogger is a big deal which forms the relationships between the blogger and everyone else.

Blog followers will follow each other too, giving opinions and recipes, as they chat and complain, all the while forming the community that makes the blog tick.

Some bloggers use Amazon for an easy way to offer shopping for their followers. Some bloggers have job boards that allow their followers to browse job opportunities. Are you starting to catch on? Blogs have ideas and solutions that people need, and innovations that can get interest going for themselves and others. Ideas get shared, and then acted upon.

Some bloggers become known for their blogs and the expertise that they bring to the table. Some are asked to be speakers at events relating to the topic of the blog, and there is extra revenue for being the speaker.

You can see that the sky is the limit, and that blogging is still a wide open field. All you have to do is to start, and see where the blogging adventure takes you.

Chapter 16: How To Utilize Wordpress For Profitable Blogging

Whether you have your own Wordpress blog or planning on creating one, the majority of individuals have probably thought of turning this into a way of generating a passive income online. Who doesn't want to have a blog that makes money for you, even when you sleep, or when you're on vacation? You've probably read and seen some big internet marketers make money from their blogs, but how do they do it? Is it possible, even if you're just a beginner?

The truth is turning your blog into a profitable one is achievable. You don't need to be a guru just to make money with your Wordpress blog, but you also have to understand that it takes a paramount of energy and time before this is achieved. The majority of people who are making money with their blog are those that have invested heavily – they spent money and time to get to where they are right now.

If you're interested, you have to become prepared. You can't expect your blog to earn money overnight after setting it up. You need to perform SEO, build your site's value, pump its rankings up, and even build a reputation online. As a matter of fact, some starters exchange guest posts with more traditional blogs to gain traffic and conversions. Social media is another channel for promoting a site.

All of these online strategies, when done correctly, can bring you traffic. The rule of the thumb is that you should be able to get people to visit your blog – you can perform thorough SEO strategies, use Google's AdWords or have someone advertise for you. It's up to you. Now that you are aware of the basic methods of attracting people to visit your blog, how can traffic turn your simple site into a profitable one?

One of the great things about having a Wordpress blog is that it is easily customizable. You can use various plug-ins, and take advantage of these plug-ins to help you with monetization. Listed below are some examples on how you can utilize your Wordpress blog and turn it into a money making machine.

1. Build A Membership Site

There is no denying that a membership site is one of the best ways to make money with your blog. This is one simple way of converting your traffic into paying members. What do they need to pay for? It depends on you.

What are your strengths? What's your niche? Many blogs offer exclusive training, e-books, seminars, tutorials, and the only way they could access these materials is by becoming a member. If you have videos that you own, exclusive content or even some e-books, and digital downloads available for your visitors, you can turn your blog into a membership website and utilize what you have. You can sell your content and have others pay for it if they want to view the content.

Another suggestion would be to offer more expensive subscriptions in case they wanted to access all content, including new ones that you'll be uploading. You can set up these subscription options to be made either monthly, quarterly, or annually. Simply said, if you get enough interest, you'll have recurring members paying you, given that you have established your membership site.

Tip: you can use a number of WordPress plugins for membership sites. Some will help you create membership logins after payment has been made, some other plugins have e-commerce solutions. You can find a membership site plugin, or an affiliate plugin – whichever is required for the site you're planning on creating.

2. Use Google AdSense

If a membership site doesn't appeal to you, but you love posting content, whether images, videos or articles, then you can apply for a Google AdSense account and get compensated every ad impression or click. This method is ideal for beginners, as the only thing that you need to setup is to add the code to your Wordpress blog. Google AdSense would then display advertisements from other businesses related to your keywords. Whenever you have a visitor or someone clicks on those ads, you'll get paid for it. Once you accumulate the threshold amount, that's the time that you'll get paid.

3. Make Use Of Affiliate Products

This was explained in more details in Chapter 13 earlier. While you have your AdSense setup, you can also become an affiliate marketer and use your blog to promote your affiliate products. For instance, if your blog is all about health and fitness, you can look for a wide range of affiliate products in the market related to health (diet supplements, exercise machines, etc.) and offer them on your blog. When someone buys them from your link, you get a commission from the retailer of those products.

While beginners tend to use multiple affiliate products and display it on their blog, it is ideal that you use one affiliate product per blog. As soon as you're making money out of your existing one, don't hesitate to invest in other domains because, in the long run, this will pay off.

4. Survey Forms Make A Great Money-Making Strategy

Have you ever downloaded content from the internet, but in order to unlock that content, you filled up a survey form? Some people find it annoying, but if you don't mind, you can setup these survey forms and you'll get paid for every completed survey. Think of content, product or something that people would want to download. It must be related to your blog or niche, of course. Join one of the survey sites, and make sure that you check their threshold amount for payouts, as well as the payment method.

5. Offer Your Own Products / Services

Lastly, if you were able to establish your own brand name in the market and happened to offer your own products and/or services, why not utilize your blog to promote your business? Many internet marketers and business people prefer using WordPress over other platforms because it is easily customizable. Turning a WordPress blog into profit-making machine can be achieved with the right strategies and with ample time and effort spent.

Do you now know what to do with your WordPress blog? Try some of these suggestions and you might just wake up and notice that your site is already generating passive income for you.

About the author

Robert B. Newhall owns several successful online businesses using the techniques taught in this eBook. Robert also loves to teach others how to be successful online working from the comfort of their own home either part-time or full-time.